SCARED?

To Isla
from

Isla

Other Books by Neal Zetter

Bees in My Bananas

Gorilla Ballerina

Here Come the Superheroes

Invasion of the Supervillains

It's Not Fine to Sit on a Porcupine

Odd Socks!

SSSSNAP! Mister Shark

When the Bell Goes

With Joshua Seigal

Yuck and Yum

SCARED?

Poems by Neal Zetter & Joshua Seigal

Illustrations by Zoe Williams

troika

Published by TROIKA
First published 2022

Troika Books Ltd, Well House, Green Lane, Ardleigh CO7 7PD, UK

www.troikabooks.com

Poems by Neal Zetter (NZ) Text copyright © Neal Zetter 2022
Poems by Joshua Seigal (JS) Text copyright © Joshua Seigal 2022

Illustrations copyright © Zoe Williams 2022
The moral rights of the authors and illustrator have been asserted

A CIP catalogue record for this book is available

from the British Library
ISBN 978-1-912745-14-2
1 3 5 7 9 10 8 6 4 2

Printed and bound in Poland at Totem.com.pl

Contents

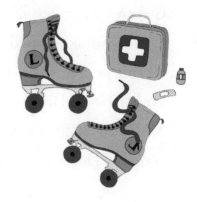

Scared?

I'm not scared of...
Creepy hairy caterpillars
Chest-beating escaped gorillas
Telling people I've been crying
Or my Uncle David dying
Mister Rankle (shouty teacher)
'Zombie Doomsday' (horror feature)

I'm not scared of...
Prickly spiky falling conkers
Towering trees like massive monsters
Bonfire Night's exploding rockets
Finding squashed slugs in my pockets
Skating on the ice in winter
Digging out a wooden splinter

I'm not scared of...

Starting school on Monday morning

Thunder with no lightning warning

Heights of mountains, depths of valleys

Walking down deserted alleys

Bothersome big boils and blisters

Cinderella's ugly sisters

But I am scared of...

When I can no longer pretend

And must admit that I'm scared

To all my family and friends

NZ

The Darker Side

We are all spectrums
Colours, tints, tones
We are all rainbows
Not grey monochrome

Endless emotions
Stirred into stews
We display bright ones
But bury the blues

Outside it's sunshine
Radiant light
Inside it's winter
Cold, bleak, bitter night

So look in a mirror
Eyes open wide
Lift up that mask and...
Meet your darker side

NZ

BUGBEARS!

We'll hide your things, mess up your bed
We'll tinker round inside your head
So you forget what you've just said
Who are we?
We're the **BUGBEARS!**

We'll fill your apple up with pips
Put sawdust in your fish and chips
Then take your teddy to the tip
Who are we?
We're the **BUGBEARS!**

Launching a surprise assault
We'll switch the sugar with the salt
With fingers fleet as thunderbolts
Who are we?
We're the **BUGBEARS!**

We'll smudge some dog dirt on your soles

We'll grab your ball and score own goals

Not elves nor pixies, dwarfs nor trolls

Who are we?

We're the **BUGBEARS!**

We're just a simple fact of life

We'll run amok, make chaos rife

We'll dance on your keyboard aaFs
jonfda'jnjfeojnoweef'pi'jffq
w8wefjbwe;jkwdoiqwr077[d
jkd89&**

Who are we?

We're the **BUGBEARS!**

JS

Gifted?

I'm good with puzzles
but I can't decipher the
rules of the playground

I'm good with numbers
but I just can't count the times
I've sat by myself

I can spell long words
but the faces that stare back
are books I can't read

They call me 'gifted'
but I can't untie the bow
that keeps me wrapped tight

On the Rack

My arms are getting longer
and my legs are snapping out.
My fingers are extending
and I feel like I could shout.

My nose is getting torn apart.
My shoulder's being strained.
I can't stand up and move about:
it seems that I am chained.

My chest is being tightened.
I can hear my ribcage pop.
My neck is getting strangled
and I wish that it would stop.

My body's being lengthened.
I know it seems far-fetched,
but yesterday my teacher told me
that I should be stretched.

JS

Haunted House

There are werewolves in the living room who
Howl! Howl! HOWL!
There are beasties in the bathroom hear them
Growl! Growl! GROWL!

In the graveyard lurk the zombies not quite
Dead! Dead! DEAD!
If you're passing through be careful where you
Tread! Tread TREAD!

Mummies resting in their coffins rattle
Chains! Chains! CHAINS!
In the kitchen ghosts and ghouls are baking
Brains! Brains! BRAINS!

In the dining room a vampire's drinking
Blood! Blood! BLOOD!
Poltergeists prowl in the basement banging
Thud! Thud! THUD!

Wicked wizards in the tower weave their
Spells! Spells! SPELLS!
Evil witches mix their stinky potion
Smells! Smells! SMELLS!
And the belfry's full of freaky flapping
Bats! Bats! BATS!
While the sewers run with scary squeaky
Rats! Rats! RATS!

Spiders hang upon the rooftop spinning
Webs! Webs! WEBS!
From the stairwell slime is dripping on your
Head! Head! HEAD!

Now a storm cloud is erupting with a
Crack! Crack! CRACK!
So I'm leaving in a hurry won't be
Back! Back! BACK!

NZ

Shadow

It follows me
and yet it's not a part of me.
It does the things I do

and yet remains
a darker hue.
What is this thing

that stretches and contorts
and shapes itself
to my movements,

that seems to know me
so intimately?
Who is this spectre

that wraps around
my presence
like a whisper?

Shadow — I would love
to get to know you
but when I reach for you

you somehow slide away
ethereally
like the final note

of some escaping melody.

JS

The World's Wickedest Dentist

I recline in her chair
Thinking life isn't fair
As I try to prepare
For the ultimate scare
She digs deep in that hole
She can no longer fill
I'm caught in the clutches of Mrs Drill

While my racing heart beats
I'm admitting defeat
Regret thousands of sweets
Cakes and sugary treats
Cos inflicting great pain
Always gives her a thrill
I'm caught in the clutches of Mrs Drill

She holds open my mouth
It's a wrestling bout
Though I yell, scream and shout
My tooth needs taking out
She says 'This shouldn't hurt'
But I know that it will
I'm caught in the clutches of Mrs Drill

Now she's numbing my gum
And enjoying her fun
With the worst yet to come
I cry 'I want my Mum!'
Instruments in her hand
Closing in for the kill
I'm caught in the clutches of Mrs Drill...

NZ

Catastrophic

The vase is on the floor again.
The bed is in a state.
The cushions have been torn apart.
The chaos won't abate.

The television's on its side,
its wires all askew.
The radiator's leaking
and there's nothing I can do.

The picture frames are cracked and bust.
The rug has been demolished.
The living room is upside down;
all calm has been abolished.

My books are torn. I feel forlorn.
My mood is rather flat.
I didn't know all this would happen
when I got a cat.

JS

Heaven

Heaven

I just don't get it

Mum tells me that it's up in the sky
Although...
I can't find it on any map
I can't find it when I search Dad's car's GPS
I can't find it even when stargazing through my new telescope

But some folk say it's all around
And if they can see it then why can't I?
Especially as I know lots of people living there
Grandad Bob
Nanny T
Aunties Em and Debs
Mr Sharma from two doors down
Mrs Achebe who used to serve our school dinners
And, apparently, Rocky, my mate Tilly's pet
salamander

I should imagine it's a pretty crowded place!
When a person goes to heaven
Everyone cries and is very upset
Yet it's supposed to be a perfect, peaceful, paradise
So is that why my many friends and relations
who have gone to heaven
Never come back?

Heaven
I just don't get it

NZ

Clowns are Evil

Clowns are evil
Clowns are bad
Clowns make me angry
Clowns make me mad

They're the most annoying creatures
in the whole human race
with all that silly powder
smeared on their face.
With stupid checkered trousers
and big flappy shoes,
I want to punch them on the nose
and give them a bruise
because

Clowns are evil
Clowns are bad
Clowns make me angry
Clowns make me mad

I hate those silly wigs they wear;
they make me want to cry.
I want to splat them in the face
with a custard pie.

They are about as funny
as a baby's dirty nappy.
They do not make me laugh
and they do not make me happy
because

Clowns are evil
Clowns are bad
Clowns make me angry
Clowns make me mad

So if you have a party
let me say to you:
you can have a magician,
you can go to the zoo,
you can serve up lovely jelly
that was made by your mum,
but if there is a clown there
I WILL NOT COME!
Because

Clowns are evil
Clowns are bad
Clowns make me angry
Clowns make me mad

Yes clowns are EVIL!
Clowns are BAD!
Clowns make me ANGRY!
Clowns make me MAD!

JS

Author's Advice

Do you want to be a better writer?

Then never be nervous

Afraid

Apprehensive

Anxious

Jittery

Jumpy

Concerned

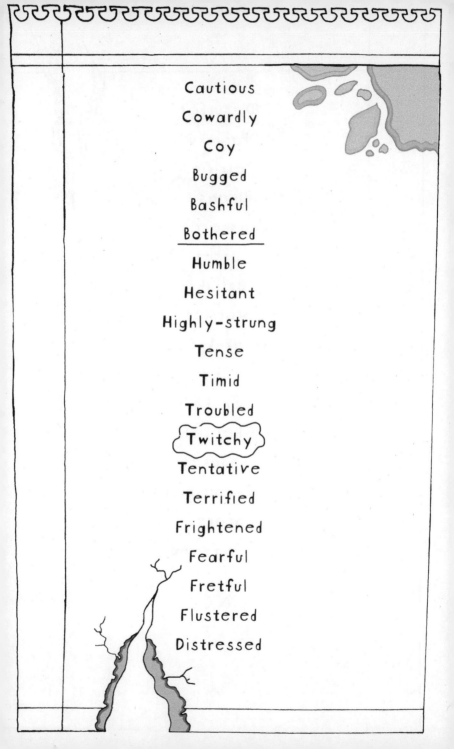

Cautious

Cowardly

Coy

Bugged

Bashful

Bothered

Humble

Hesitant

Highly-strung

Tense

Timid

Troubled

Twitchy

Tentative

Terrified

Frightened

Fearful

Fretful

Flustered

Distressed

Disturbed

Panicky

≥ Petrified ≤

Uneasy

Unassertive

Upset

Uptight

Worried

Weak-kneed

Shy

Shaky

Sheepish

Spooked

Self-conscious

Scared

About using synonyms

NZ

Marbles

I keep them locked
in a box by my bed.

I will never let anybody
have the key.

Grandpa says the only thing
he truly fears
is losing his marbles

so at least I know now
that I won't
lose mine.

JS

Bully!

Gonna mash you up like strawberry jam

Gonna use your head as a battering ram

Gonna kick your rucksack as hard as I can

I'm a mixed-up man

With an odious plan

What am I?

You're a bully!

Gonna nick your phone

Gonna pull your hair

Gonna cuss your mum

Mock the clothes you wear

I'm a vicious, vindictive sore-headed bear

Push in the dinner queue — if you dare

What am I?

You're a bully!

I can be racist

I can spit bile

I can be a fascist

And totally vile

I'm your judge, your jury
With no fair trail
And if I don't use violence
I'll hurt you with what I say
About your culture, race, religion
Or being gay
I'm a vulture
You're my prey
Oi! Get outta my way!
What am I?
You're a bully!

It's cos I've got no friends you see
That I bully to hide my insecurity
In fact people used to bully me
So now I'll make your life a misery
What am I?
You're a bully!

NZ

Circle Time

We have it every Friday.
We go round one by one
taking turns to say
what's on our mind.

Yesterday James discussed
visiting France this summer.
Ahmad talked about his new baby sister;
Ruth spoke of her kitten.

I said nothing. Again.
Just stared at the swirls
on the carpet and shrugged.
Miss Ellis said I didn't have to talk
if I didn't want.

And I wish I could tell them.
I wish I could explain

how Dad and Laura
fight in the night
when they think I'm sleeping.

I wish I could talk
of that tangled twine
that tightens round my torso
when they fire those poison arrows.

But I said nothing. Again.
Just kept my eyes down
as that still small voice
murmured once more
how it's all my fault.

JS

My Mummy is a Mummy

My mummy is a mummy,

linen-wrapped from toe to head

She sleeps in a sarcophagus instead of in a bed

She's not keen on the daytime

cos she's frightened of the light

The bits of her you'd recognise are

hidden out of sight

While most of us use bandages
for grazes and for cuts
She uses them for fashion
and I think that's pretty nuts
Her fondness for Egyptian culture
cannot be denied
Last week she bought a pyramid
and made her home inside

My mummy is a mummy -
it's incredible yet true
She hopes to meet the pharaohs,
sphinx and Cleopatra too
It's very complicated
when she's taking baths or showers
Her skin's a mess and getting dressed
can take her several hours

Though Mum says that it didn't hurt
when she was first embalmed
She often finds it difficult
to move her legs and arms
I shouted, 'Dad, this is so mad
and also it's not right'
But he's not fussed cos he becomes...
a werewolf every night!

NZ

Giving

After Roger McGough

I give you rain to grow your crops
You give me pain that never stops
I give you light to show the way
You give me blight and cause decay

I give you trees to aid your breath
You give disease and summon death
I give you vines that bear you fruit
You dig your mines and you pollute

I give you fauna great and small
You give disorder to it all
I give you earth on which to grow
You give me dearth and bring me woe

I give you shores on which to stand
You give me wars and burn the land
I give my word for you to heed
So please be spurred, for I'm in need.

JS

Carbon Footprint

I'm your deadly carbon footprint
Lurking spectre grim and grey
Growing larger, never smaller
I will never fade away
Stalking stealthily behind you
While you live your life on Earth
I'm your stain, your deep impression
I'm your legacy, your curse

I'm your dirty carbon footprint

Don't ignore my warning sign

I'm your carelessness, your cancer

Soon consuming humankind

As you use your power electric

Coal and petrol, oil and gas

Killing nature with pollution

While you're counting up your cash

I'm your lethal carbon footprint

Leaving you a bitter taste

Eating up all of our planet

Thriving on your piles of waste

I'm your rubbish not recycled

I'm the sting that's in your tail

If you want to see tomorrow

Then you need to shrink me... now!

NZ

Monkey on My Back

There's a monkey
There's a monkey
There's a monkey on my back.

No matter where I try to go
the monkey comes with me.
He wraps his legs around me
like he's hanging from a tree.
He throws things at my teachers
and he bellows at my friends.
I need to make him go away!
I need to make amends.

There's a monkey
There's a monkey
There's a monkey on my back.

The monkey shares a bed with me,
he has his own pyjamas.
He makes my bedroom dirty
with the skins of old bananas.
My parents kicked me out the house,
the monkey made them cross.
I'm desperate to get rid of him,
he needs to know who's boss.

There's a monkey
There's a monkey
There's a monkey on my back.

The monkey's getting cumbersome.
He's really quite a weight!
He's hairy and he's smelly
and he makes me feel irate.
He doesn't even let up
when I'm sitting on the loo.
My heart feels like a jungle
and my head feels like a zoo!

There's a monkey

There's a monkey

There's a monkey on my back.

JS

I Don't Like Sssssssnakes

The way they feel, the way they bite
The way they curl up very tight
The way they slither 'cross the ground
The way they slide without a sound
I don't...
Like...
Sssssssnakes

The way their tongues are shaped like forks
The way they never smile or talk
The way they have no hair at all
The way they cannot kick a ball
I don't...
Like...
Sssssssnakes

The way they're still until they strike
The way they're rubbish riding bikes
The way there's poison in their fangs
The way they hang about in gangs

I don't...
Like...
Ssssssnakes

The way they shed their scaly skins
The way they look so long and thin
The way they hide inside your bed
The way they might prefer you dead
I don't...
Like...
Ssssssnakes

Cobra, rattlesnake or adder
Grass snake, python or black mamba
Boa constrictor or sidewinder
Anaconda or pit viper...
I don't...
Like...
Sssssssssssssnakesssssssssssss!

NZ

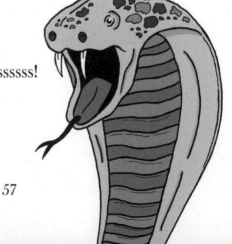

Max is Not in School

Today the sun shines
a little bit brighter.
Today the wind has lost
its bite, and the air
hangs less heavy
in the classroom.

Today Max
is not in school.

Today my ears are not stung
by barbed words.
Today my ribs don't tighten
in my chest
as taunts lash out
across the playground.

Today my books
are in my bag
and not torn up and scattered
across the floor.
There's a small oasis
in the wide parched desert,
a faint rainbow
in the winter storm.

Today I can breathe
just for a while

because Max
is not in school.

JS

Not a Vampire

Red sticky stuff upon my lips
Is strawberry jam
The razor teeth I'm sharpening
Are toy fake fangs
I dress in swish black velvet suits
So I look smart
Nobody's tried to drive a stake
Into my heart

You say that crosses bother me
Well that's not true
The only bats I've ever known
Are at the zoo
I'm cool with mirrors in my house
And garlic's fine
That zombie living down the street's
No mate of mine

As I won't sunbathe on the beach
My skin's snow white
I promise you I'm sound asleep
Before midnight
Thick fog around my castle
Is a morning mist
Count Dracula is fictional
He don't exist

No need to cover up your neck
When you meet me
I wouldn't drink your human blood
I'd opt for tea
Those trips to Transylvania?
I've never been
I'm really NOT a vampire
It's just your bad dream

NZ

Gone Off Milk

gone off milk
foul and thick

gone off milk
makes me sick

gone off milk
in my bowl

gone off milk
rots my soul

gone off milk
in my cup

gone off milk

might throw up

gone off milk

what a stink

gone off milk

down the sink

gone off milk

here's my vow:

I've gone off milk

forever now!

JS

Exclamation Mark!

Compelled to shriek! and shout! aloud
Not born to blend in with the crowd
I stand up straight and tall and proud
Muscular, mighty
You don't want to fight me
I'm an exclamation mark!

I must be noticed, must be seen
Forget those letters in between
My power boosts your every scream!
Not fancy, not fluffy
A roughie, a toughie
I'm an exclamation mark!

Scare commas, colons and full stops

Cause shocked apostrophes to drop

Ellipses to lose all their dots

An upstart, a raver

Unruly behaviour

I'm an exclamation mark!

I'll amplify a **zoooom!** for you

Whizzzz! boooom! bash! crash!

enhance them too

Or even **cock-a-doodle-doo!**

I'm craving attention

So once more I'll mention

I'm an exclamation mark!!!!!

NZ

When Dad Turns into an Incredible Hulk

He rips his jeans
His shirt and vest
Lets out a ROOOOAAAAR!
Then beats his chest
My sister shrieks, my mother sulks
When Dad turns into an incredible hulk

Displaying strength
That's quite obscene
White skin transforms
To emerald green
If angered there's just one result
When Dad turns into an incredible hulk

Feet stomp and stamp
Legs leap and bound
Tall buildings fall
From all around
His muscles bulge, his body bulks
When Dad turns into an incredible hulk

The neighbours hide
Shops have to close
Gales gust and whoosh
Tornadoes blow
Our road is full of frightened folk
When Dad turns into an incredible hulk

He'll kick and punch
Smash, thrash and hit
My bedroom's broken
Left in bits
It rarely is a good result
When Dad turns into an incredible hulk

His fuse is lit
His temper's gone
A sonic boom
An atom bomb
We wish he was a normal bloke
When Dad turns into an incredible hulk

Why does he rage?
Nobody's sure
The doctors say
'There is no cure!'
Call 999 cos it's no joke
When Dad turns into an incredible hulk

NZ

Computer Bug

I'm a nasty little computer bug
Nibble, nosh, crunch!
Eating your computer when it's time for lunch
Gnawing through the circuits
While I lick my lips
I'll hack you
I'll attack you
Gobble up those microchips

I'm demolishing your new mobile phone
Slobber, slurp, bite!
I trick you to invite me in then I strike
Smashing every socket
Slowing down your screen
I'll creep up
I will sneak up
Melt your programmes like ice cream

I'm invading your tablet and laptop too

Dribble, burp, yum!

Chewing through your favourite game fills my tum

Feasting on your keyboard

Messing with your mouse

The direst

Of viruses

You'll fail to flush me out

You can install security software

Disconnect all plugs

But you'll never defeat this nasty little computer bug

NZ

The Internet
is Watching

It knows the times
you sleep and wake,
and when you work
or take a break,
and every choice
you ever make —
the internet is watching.

It clocks the things
you say and do,
with prying eyes
it spies on you
and launches a
surveillance coup —
the internet is watching.

It tracks you with
its laser sight,
observing you
both day and night.
Forever trapped,
you can't take flight —
the internet is watching.

Its pincers poke
inside your brain.
You can't opt out;
you can't abstain.
So watch your back
and don't complain —
the internet is watching.

JS

Hierarchy of Terror

1. Going to the dentist

2. Failing my science exam

3. Making mistakes when I write lists

5. Mutant guinea pigs

6. Empty spaces

7.

8. Getting lost in a forest at night (with bears)

9. Being forced, at gunpoint, to go snorkelling in the crater of a bubbling volcano

10. Growing up.

JS

the d   I   vorce

dad kept the big car	mum kept the small car
dad kept the computer	mum kept the laptop
dad kept the motorbike	mum kept the mountain bike
dad kept the records and cds	apart from mum's take that albums
dad kept the dog	mum kept the cat
dad kept his books	mum kept her books
dad moved out of london	mum stayed there

and ME?

NZ

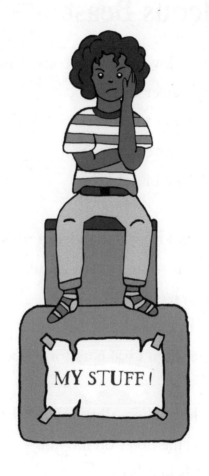

My Mum is in Love with a Hideous Beast

My mum is in love with a hideous beast.
It only comes over at night.
When I'm under my covers
I hear the two lovers,
kissing away out of sight.

My mum is in love with a hideous troll
or perhaps it is some kind of ghoul.
Round about ten o'clock
I hear keys in the lock,
but it's gone when I wake up for school.

I find little love letters all round the flat
and strange little notes on the wall –
the beast calls her 'honey'
and 'darling sweet bunny'!
I don't like this creature at all.

Why isn't mum scared out of her wits?
Why doesn't she wail and yell?
If it came in my room
I'd grab a big broom
and I'd bludgeon its brains to hell!

So I asked my mum about the beast,
she said there's no need to get mad.
She said I was foolish,
the creature's not ghoulish –
she said it was only my dad.

My mum is in love with a curious man
and it seems that at last I know who:
my dad left those letters.
If I knew him better
then maybe I'd love my dad too.

JS

Yesterday My Head Exploded

Yesterday my head exploded with a loud
KA-BOOM!
Wanted to learn maths but found there wasn't
any room
Couldn't fit more knowledge in
Now my neck is just a chin

Yesterday my head exploded with a loud
KER-SPLAT!
Leaving me an empty space right underneath
my hat
Tried to squeeze in one new fact
Straw that broke the camel's back

Yesterday my head exploded with a loud
KA-POW!
Lost my ears, my nose, my mouth, my teeth, my hair,
my brow

While my friends looked on and laughed
I sat headless in the class

Yesterday my head exploded with a loud
KER-RUNCH!
Had to stop my studying, unable to
eat lunch
Too much work too little play
Caused my top to blow away

Yesterday my head exploded with a loud
KER-POP!
As my brain has disappeared this poem has to...
STOP!

NZ

Averse

I've no time for rhymes
Shape poems are worse
Haiku are horrible
Kennings a curse

I loathe limericks, acrostics
Sonnets, cinquains, odes
Lyrics, raps and ballads
Because I am a poetryphobe

NZ

Back to School

A notable thing
That the tale of three small words
Can hold such a sting.

JS

Tyrannosaurus Came to Tea

(Inspired by the late Judith Kerr, author of
The Tiger Who Came to Tea.)

Tyrannosaurus came to tea

Chaos!
Catastrophe!

Bashing down the kitchen door

Cracking tiles on our floor

Mum warned us that there'd be trouble

Living room's a pile of rubble

Tyrannosaurus came to tea

Nightmare!
Calamity!

Smashing every single plate

Leaving our house in a state

Scoffed the fridge then stuffed the freezer

Really quite a greedy geezer

Tyrannosaurus came to tea

Bedlam!
Pure anarchy!

Snarling through his gnashing teeth
Spreading dread, distress and grief
Said his favourite meal was curry
'Seconds' he roared 'And please hurry!'

Tyrannosaurus came to tea

Disaster!
Tragedy!

Not a very good idea
Prehistoric monster here
Knives and forks are bent and busted
This guy clearly can't be trusted

Tyrannosaurus came to tea

Police!
Emergency!

Took the roof off when he stretched
Home is now a total wreck
Fortunately he ignored us
The moral...
NEVER feed a tyrannosaurus!

NZ

The Tiger

doesn't want you
to look into her eyes.

You can marvel at her stance
and the way her tongue flicks
across her fangs;

you can cower at her claws
and the stripes that streak
like poison down her back;

you can even draw up close
to catch her bitter breath
but the tiger doesn't want you
to look into her eyes

for
should you do so
you might see nothing more
than another little housecat
        blinking
                back at you.

JS

Skeleton in
the Cupboard

I've a skeleton in the cupboard
Who's looking rather thin
And all alone
Composed of bone
Devoid of any skin

He dangles on a hanger
Reveals a faceless stare
It's no surprise, he has no eyes
No heart, no brain, no hair

I've a skeleton in the cupboard
He's simply known as Fred
Stuck in a pose
Not wearing clothes
And absolutely dead

A corpse is in the closet
But cut the gloom and doom
We often chat and chew the fat
From midnight until noon

I've a skeleton in the cupboard
Above my shoes and socks
Although deceased
I'm begging please
Don't notify the cops

And tell them of my secret
Because my lifeless pal
Is chilled and cool and as a rule
Is happy anyhow

Now if you think this poem's title's just a metaphor
I suggest you visit my bedroom, then...
Carefully...
Open the cupboard door...

NZ

Untitled

Today I woke up
without my soul
where it should have been –
just a gaping hole.
But I didn't despair
or cry or shout,
for there's nothing there
to care about.

JS

Nobody Knows This

but just beneath my skin
a volcano is preparing
to blast.

Behind these eyes,
inside the prison
of my ribs, magma
bubbles silently.

Smoke is filling
the cavern of my lungs
as fire flicks the basement
of my tongue.

As I sit still
to write these words,
nobody knows this.

But they soon will.

JS

Sadness

When Sadness came around to play
He frightened Happiness away
He knocked me flat with just a punch
He ate my laughter for his lunch
He threatened me for far too long
As I surrendered he grew strong

When Sadness knocked upon my door
My heavy heart fell to the floor
Creating night-time in my day
Why was he here? He wouldn't say
He squashed my spirit, zip and zest
My mean and uninvited guest

When Sadness sneaked into my room
He spread his sorrow, doom and gloom
My teardrops dripped down from my eyes
I couldn't fight him though I tried
He bullied me, he fuelled my fears
Then for no reason disappeared

I don't know when he'll next attack
But one thing's certain...he'll be back

NZ

Something Down the Plughole

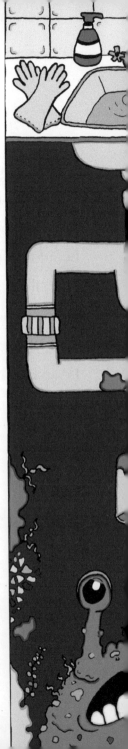

There's something down the plughole
There's something down the sink
I felt a claw and saw a paw
While at the tap to drink

A weird and eerie creature
Composed of sludge and slime
It crawled up from the sewage pipe
And feeds on grease and grime

Emitting awful odours
It hasn't got a name
The Beastie from the Basin?
The Demon from the Drain?

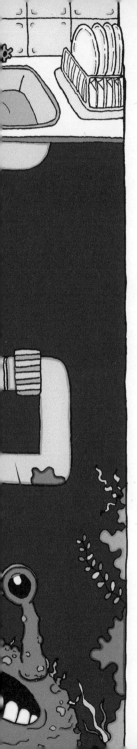

Who knows if it is friendly
Or if it might attack?
Be careful when you're washing up
In case it wants a snack!

We pushed it with a plunger
We poked it with a knife
But still it stays, won't go away
The lurker in our pipe

We're hearing burps at midnight
We're hearing slurps at dawn
So enter our kitchen at your own risk
Don't say you've not been warned...

NZ

Black Holes

Black holes are lurking everywhere Not just in outer space One swallowed my maths homework Then left without a trace

Snatched my sprouts today And possibly grabbed stranded last year When he went away The black hole by the dinner table

My lost socks are on Neptune Cos a black hole took them too They ate the keeper feeding lions Lunchtime at the zoo

Black holes steal all my self-control If my behaviour's bad Remove my hopes and happiness If I'm upset or sad

Dad says black holes consume our cash
Each time mum goes to shop
They gobble up the sunshine also
Making summers stop

Beware these holes are all around
Deep, endless, dark and black
And anything they suck inside
Might NOT be coming back!

NZ

The Orange Table

I sit on the Orange Table.
Not the Red or Blue or Green.
This is where Miss has put me
and I think I know what it means.

It means my writing's not too good.
It means I cannot spell.
I don't know if they know I know
but I only know too well.

I sit on the Orange Table.
It's where I've sat all year.
I can't do Maths or Science
they say, and so they put me here.

I'm not so hot at school work,
which means I'm not too smart
so I sit on the Orange Table
so I can be kept apart.

I sit on the Orange Table.
They say that this is best.
But they can't see the orange fire
that burns inside my chest.

JS

My Secret Is

the burning orb behind my eyes
the robber donning his disguise

the dagger poised above my head
the centipede beneath the bed

the paw prints of some distant bear
the creaking of a rocking chair

the cackle heard across the plain
the twisting of a dusty lane

the nameless baby in a well
the thing that I can never tell

JS

One Breaktime
I Got Married

One breaktime I got married.
The class all gathered round.
The eagerness was palpable,
the gaiety profound.

I gave my bride a flower.
We then exchanged an oath.
The priest proclaimed us wedded
and then sanctified us both.

Alas it wasn't meant to last.
Things didn't go to plan.
She took away my conkers
then she ran away with Dan.

The course of love is bumpy.
At least that is my hunch.
One breaktime I got married
and we got divorced by lunch.

JS

L Plates

I broke both legs
Smashed several toes
I grazed my knees
Fractured my nose
I hit my head
I split my lip
Then jarred my jaw
And sprained my hip

I burst my lungs
Ruptured my spleen
Bruised all my back
Black, blue and green
I crushed my arm
I cracked my wrist
Lost two front teeth
(Still sorely missed)

My elbow's chipped

My ankle's numb

It hurts me to

Sit on my bum

My shoulder snapped

My spine is strained

I'm not gonna roller-skate again

NZ

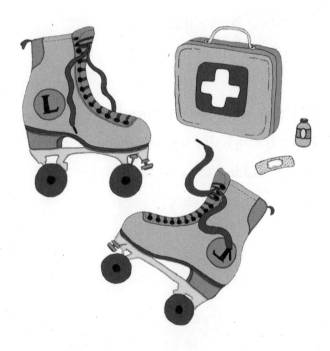

Living in the Future

I zip to school on strips of light
My super specs augment my sight
Remote controls adjust my height —
I'm living in the future.

I eat my dinner in a pill
No viruses can make me ill
My iPhone 30 is a thrill —
I'm living in the future.

My DNA has been enhanced
By microchips that are advanced
My new IQ leaves you entranced —
I'm living in the future.

Those past travails have been and gone
A brave new world? Just bring it on!
I'm proud to carry the baton
For living in the future.

But here I am, without a friend
My mum and dad have met their end
So stop this game! Let's not pretend
I'm living in the future...

JS

The Seriously Scary Poem

This poem is deadly
Dark, horrible, heavy
Grey, grisly, gruesome and grim
It's frighteningly fearful
Could leave you quite tearful
It does what it says on the tin

This poem's doom-laden
Don't read it to children
Or when you're alone by yourself
It may melt your ice creams
Cause nightmares and bad dreams
And certainly damage your health

This poem's not comic
You'll find no jokes in it
Devoid of all humour and cheer
It's hideous, hated
Now treble-X-rated
Most strenuous, strict and severe

This poem is solemn
Repulsive and rotten
I bet you're already depressed
Mean, miserable, manic
And sure to spread panic
Don't you like the funny ones best?

NZ

Lullaby

There are faces
in the way the curtains fall.
There are faces
in the shadows on the wall.
There are faces
on the carpet, on the floor.
There are faces
right outside the bedroom door.

Watch them grimace,
watch them sneer
as you're cowering in fear.

There are fingers
tapping on the window pane.
There are fingers
reaching right inside your brain.
There are fingers

poking from the chest of drawers.
There are fingers,
far too many to ignore.

Feel them reaching,
feel them prying,
they will grab if you start crying.

There are voices
in the clicking of the light.
There are voices
in the gentle hush of night.
There are voices
in the crackle of the trees.
There are voices
in the cackle of the breeze,

and they're coming straight from hell.
So nighty-night then.
Sleep well...

JS

Neal Zetter
Poet

Neal Zetter has been writing, performing and even dreaming about poetry since he was six years old - Roman times, as he regularly tells children - so it's no wonder that this is his 11th book. His sparkling poetry career has included winning the Silver Book Award, being acclaimed by the Reading Agency and BookTrust, having his work featured on London buses and in the Guardian and London Standard newspapers. He has performed his adult poems in the Royal Festival Hall, at a League 2 football match, festivals, weddings and funerals (really), countless top West End comedy clubs and hosted his own club for ten years. Since 1994, Neal has staged his fun poetry-writing workshops in hundreds of schools and libraries in the UK and beyond, teaching 3-103 year olds to create their own fantastic poetry. Despite rumours, Joshua Seigal is neither Neal's son nor his brother.

See more about Neal at his website:
www.cccpworkshops.co.uk

Joshua Seigal
Poet

Joshua Seigal wrote his first poem when he was five years old. It was about otters, and it wasn't very good. Thankfully Joshua's work has improved since then, and he has been a professional poet for the last decade. As well as taking one-man shows to the Edinburgh Festival, Joshua has performed in far-flung places such as Italy, Belgium, India, China, Turkey and Margate, some of these performances being online, in the comfort of his own living room. Joshua has won numerous awards, including The Laugh Out Loud award and The People's Book Prize, has written and performed for BBC television, and is an official ambassador for National Poetry Day. He can normally be found visiting schools (or anywhere that'll have him, really); his favourite animal is a lemur and his least favourite food is cottage cheese. Despite being neither Neal's brother nor his son, he has developed a kind of grudging respect for him nonetheless.

See more about Joshua at his website:
www.joshuaseigal.co.uk

Zoe Williams
Illustrator

A recent graduate from Bath Spa University, *Scared?* is Zoe's first published work of illustrations (and she's very excited about it!). An aspiring artist from day one, Zoe could always be found drawing, creating, and thinking about new ideas. She received a sixth-form arts scholarship, which inspired her to illustrate stories herself, focusing on her love of drawing by creating quirky characters and scenarios. Defined by line, tone, and a sense of charm, this selection of Zoe's work is an exciting debut of what's to come. Having received an honours degree in English Literature and Publishing, she is now off to Bristol to study a Masters in Graphic Arts. Zoe plans to pursue a career as a freelance illustrator and hopes to contribute to more books in future (scary and otherwise).

See more about Zoe at her website:
www.zoewilliamsillustration.com

troika

The home of great children's books

Troika is a small independent children's
book publisher. We're based in the UK.

Follow us on social media

 @TroikaBooks

 @troikabooks

 @Troika